Born Premature, Loved Overdue

Born Premature, Loved Overdue

A Memoir of Survivor's Guilt, Neglect and Abuse

R. Antonio Matta

Dedication

To Melody Acosta,
I express my deepest gratitude for your unwavering support and guidance through the years—clinically, professionally, and personally. 🩶 Your warmth and love have been a constant source of inspiration, and your social and emotional intelligence has helped me navigate through the most challenging times. Your wisdom has been an anchor, keeping me grounded through many adversities and changes.

Without you, I would never have been able to unearth "the truth" to write this book. Your influence has been a healing balm, and your presence has left an indelible imprint on my life.

This dedication is a tribute to you. I will forever be grateful for your role in helping me shape my destiny and help me become who I am today.

With gratitude, admiration, and love,
R. Antonio Matta

Table of Contents

Prologue

---

1 in 525 Billion Chances of a Lifetime

Bittersweet.
I'm going to miss the Sertoli cells.
They were so good to me.
Not just me; in the early days, that's where we all dwelled.
All we stem cells were kept full of nutrients and blood products, no matter how immature.
We weren't all ready for the migration, but I was ready for change.
Ready to leave behind the demure.
No validation is needed to secure a mind that has already been made up.
It's time to move on, guys.
Either get left behind or try your best to catch up.
This isn't the time to be scared.

Fear will have you ensnared.
But fear would keep us as mere germ cells, never to see
the light of day.
I don't want to miss this.
We all can't go to the epididymis.
I'm ready!
Never before have I been so.
There have been so many changes.
But the epididymis will be our rites of passage.
Let's go!
I'm quite fond of my oval-shaped head.
The other stems wouldn't believe my new tailpiece.
I'll soon be like an Olympian swimmer, gaining motility.
Rumor has it that only two-fifths of us will actually swim
on the day of destiny.
The day of the sex, consummating my optimistic dreams
of fertility.
I don't fear drowning in the seminal fluid when the flood
comes.
This Spermatogenesis is only good for two and a half
months.
Every day, millions of new guys come into these testes.
I don't care where they come from.
I got my eye on the prize.
No time to fraternize.
Only one of us can fertilize.
This has been my destiny.
My dream.
Thru the fire.
My only desire.
My purpose is to seed the creation of a new god.

Not an inferior demigod, but a divinely blessed being to walk among the other gods and goddesses.
The Most High's will be done, but yet, through my will, I'll shirk any qualms of slip shoddiness.
As a germ cell first coming into these pubescent, partially maned testicles, I knew I had staying power.
The rest is trivial.
Praying my host decides against contraception his first time to third base.
God's grace won't permit the earth another immaculate conception.
Still, somewhere in the universe, someone's giving me the nod.
No matter how stacked up the odds.
1.2 billion, to be exact.
I've battled with my doubts.
But my faith, my hope, knocked me back on track.
I know now that seeing is deceiving.
Dreaming is believing.
I believe in myself, and that is an unadulterated fact.
I confess.
This cocky confidence hasn't always been so predominant.
From a germ cell to a stem, my entire circumference once housed turbulent self-doubt and dissidence.
I never thought I'd make it out of this boy's body.
If I did, I just knew it would be in a suffocating coffin of hand lotion or a tissue flushed at sea.
But I've been visualizing.
I can see it happening differently now for me.
My dreams are becoming reality.

Right now.
It's time.
I feel it getting warm, and all around me, there's com-
motion.
It's either do or die!
My bravery is zealous, but my tail still has anxious undu-
lation.
Do I remember the route?
Don't panic; just remember the route.
First, it's through that conduit that sounds like that soul
singer.
R. E. S. P. E. C. T.
Dang, it!
What's it called?
Oh yeah, the Urethra.
How could I forget?
Then, directly into her.
Next, her cervix.
This is happening so quickly!
Think.
Ok, there's the uterus.
Then, fallopian tubes.
Finally, the ovum.
Ok, I got the route.
Now, with just the right propelling power from this kid's
final thrust.
I've got this!
I think this boy is about to blow!
Any moment now.
I can feel it.
Here comes all I got.

On your marks.
Ready.
Set.
Go.
And I'm off!
See you later, suckers!
I've got this!
Faster!
First checkpoint.
Second.
Almost there!
Third.
Fourth.
Wait, I don't believe this!
Am I in the lead?
Don't look back!
Stay the course.
Stay focused.
Swim.
Faster.
Move your two-thousandths of an-inch frame!
This is the win for the game!
Survival of the fittest!
Those poor, slow tadpoles behind me.
Yes, I did it!
I'm here now.
I'm in.
Precious egg, meet my 23 chromosomes!
Let the conception begin.
Five hundred twenty-five billion sperm cells are regener-
ated in a man's lifetime.

I'm the one that made it.
Let love bless this life so it is inspiring, empowering, and sublime.

Lemons. I love them—the fruit, not the cars. Yes. I've always loved lemons. As a kid, I would eat them raw, like oranges. I love just about all lemon by-products, too—lemon pie, lemon cookies, lemon pepper, lemon bundt cake, Lemonhead candies, lemon in my tea, and with the life I've been living all these years, I would have to love lemonade.

That idiom, "If life gives you lemons, make lemonade," commands an acquired skill. I grew up poor—not destitute, but poverty was never far away. As a way to adapt to constantly feeling like I had less than, especially around Christmas time when all the kids would return to school from winter vacation, bragging about all the new stuff they got, I quickly learned how to make less seem more. I mastered delusional thinking well before a psychiatrist labeled it as less than an auspicious trait of mental disturbance. That's how I learned to live—to survive in a world comprised of the haves and have-nots. While it kept me from feelings of privation, I did it so automatically that I never developed a sense of discernment. There's a time to kid yourself and a time to accept reality.

Most of the time, I didn't see anything at face value. Stale, sliced white bread, topped with ketchup, and curvaceously sliced Bologna became pepperoni pizza. Ramen noodles drenched in tomato paste, sprinkled with ground black pepper, and chopped chunks of mystery meat hot dogs tossed in to become spaghetti with meatballs. I loved every bite, as if these ghetto imitation Italian cuisines were the authentic dishes.

Although not clear to me until decades later, as the residual echos of silent and invisible abuse and the possibly irreversible damage from the detriment of my grandmother's emotional and custodial neglect suffocate my self-esteem and self-perception, I realize now that every breath, curdle, cry or coo I made as a ward of the state, an orphan left behind by her deceased firstborn child, bridled her hatred for me. She resented me.

Her potentially greedy motives for accepting the responsibility to raise me became a regretful burden that she took out on me relentlessly with serpentine stealth and imprecated charades so that no one knew of the horror and the contempt she felt for me as she would feed me baby formula and change diapers in the middle of the night, cursing the abomination whose very existence maliciously murdered her lovely child. I just stayed with her in the house, and she packaged me and our relationship deceptively to avoid ACS and imprisonment. For years, I was silent, and when I finally spoke, no one believed me. What appeared to be was not what it was.

Even though my eye color and skin complexion were much lighter than my mother's, I was a daily reminder of her daughter, who had been around long before me. To consolidate the various stories, my conception was the beginning of the end. My mother had cancer as a child. What kind of cancer? I don't know because no one ever talked about it like it was a dark family secret that would cause the clouds to rip apart and lightning instantly strike a person down dead if uttered.

For the longest time, I thought cancer was just cancer—like a cold was a cold, and chickenpox was chickenpox. I didn't know there were different kinds. Still, I grew up despising this malignant monster "Cancer" like it was Satan. My mother's cancer went into remission, and she was healthy for quite some time. Her doctors advised her not to become pregnant because the cancer would return.

For some reason, either my mother didn't believe the physician's warning after being well for so long, or she just wanted to risk it because she acquiesced in unprotected sex with my father. But my mother had intentions. Whatever her motives, she got pregnant, and as the doctor predicted, she got progressively ill during her pregnancy with me.

It is widely understood that unborn babies form a bond with their mothers while still in the womb, which is then later intensified with the attachment after birth. My inaccessibility to these vital connections, however, and to develop neurologically with or without minor or significant impairments was determined in the neonatal stage of my premature birth. This period would shape my future susceptibility to substance misuse or mental health issues, dictate my tendency towards forming unhealthy relationships, and influence my capacity to feel and express love, among other things.

From the first taste of a mother's milk or the comforting embrace of her arms, an infant finds security in an unfamiliar world. Alternatively, the absence of these experiences can lead to the precarious initiation of biorhythms that cyclically impact the rest of the child's life.

In my case, I was whisked away to an incubator moments after my birth, my fragile existence sustained by machines. I suspect my mother had only a fleeting moment to look at me before we were parted. Her life ended three months later. Due to my premature birth, my weight well below the average, and the loss of an entire trimester of gestation, I was deprived of one of my most fundamental needs at the earliest stage of my life: my mother's presence.

As her family mourned my mother's death, who was in the mood to celebrate my life? She left me with a mob of individuals who secretly resented my existence. Of course, no one ever said it, but actions speak decibels louder than words. For them to outwardly admit that they could never love the gift my mother gave to the world would be to blaspheme their standing in the Church. These devout, religious groups of Christians—some ministers, deacons, and evangelists—wouldn't dare. Much of my life has felt like a life sentence, but I'm innocent! I didn't mean to kill her.

I want to clarify that nothing I express in this work is intended to question my guardian's faith in God or Jesus Christ. By sharing my experiences, I hope to liberate myself from the darkness that enveloped a significant part of my life. Having traveled a long and ever-ascending path of personal development and spiritual growth, I use this work to finally free my heart from the chains of "the hurt caused by that hurt person," choosing instead to let forgiveness and gratitude govern my perspective on these painful childhood experiences.

The profound impact of adverse childhood experiences on a person's life cannot be overstated, and I hope that my words might prevent at least one abusive childhood from slipping unnoticed under the pretense of religious love. There have already been too many centuries of harm committed in the name of God.

Finally, while it may sometimes appear as though I'm vilifying my legal guardian, my broader aim is for this work to contribute to the existing literature on survivor's guilt, acknowledging that guilt complexes are as varied as human complexions and languages. Awareness of my survivor's guilt's nuanced manifestations—from self-sabotaging tendencies to isolating social anxieties—has increased. Yet, I'm still far from fully healed, and the path to total recovery may last a lifetime.

Chapter One

Although I don't have the authority to decipher the complexities of individual belief systems, my journey through a tapestry of diverse relationships and experiences has led to an eye-opening realization. On the surface, I've found that most people I've encountered possess at least a degree of self-love. This doesn't imply total self-admiration but rather sufficient self-respect that directs them toward their well-being—most of the time.

However, based on my wealth of personal interactions, I venture to suggest that if love and hate are opposite extremes of an emotional spectrum, with 'like' standing as the midpoint, many people would probably lean more towards hate yet remain grounded just shy of self-appreciation, if they were to dive deep within themselves and were honest about what they saw.

Despite the internal struggle, these individuals often avoid admitting to self-loathing, likely due to the fear of societal judgment. I, however, diverge from this group, not with a sense of superiority, but with an honest acknowledgment and acceptance of my reality. I've lived the majority of my life shrouded in illusions, pretending to be indifferent to self-hatred to preserve my time, energy, and societal image.

Our societal matrix often dissuades overt displays of hatred, considering them too extreme. Yet, if I were to deny that my self-loathing acts as a burdensome albatross, its shadow pervading my life and subtly manipulating my subconscious and thought processes, I'd be deceiving myself. My self-loathing has lessened over time, but it persists, undeterred by any measures of self-love I put into practice.

To shed light on my feelings, let's consider an analogy: If you dislike your car, would you cherish, protect, clean, invest in, or take pride in it like a vehicle you liked, even mildly? I suspect most wouldn't. They might only care enough to maintain its basic functionality for transportation. This, in a nutshell, mirrors my life's story; I've often neglected the most basic acts of self-care like bathing, brushing my teeth, or washing my clothes. I harbor a deep, unadorned hatred for myself.

I wrestled with this self-loathing for a prolonged period, perplexed by the seeming affection others had for me. After three years of introspective psychoanalysis, I had a breakthrough: I was shackled by survivor's guilt. This enlightening revelation dissipated the fog of confusion and explained my enduring deficiency of self-love.

My maternal bloodline contributed significantly to my guilt, although my paternal relatives played a more minor part. My mother, a young cancer survivor, was warned that a pregnancy could be hazardous. The circumstances of my conception, whether a passionate teen romance or an unfortunate oversight, remain unknown to me. My mother's health declined during my gestation, leading to my premature birth.

Premature births, rife with risks and uncertainties, are a subject of profound interest. In addition to missing a trimester of vital development, my birth was surrounded by significant events. Immediately after exiting the womb, I experienced clinical death. After resuscitation, respiratory distress syndrome followed— a common condition among preemies. Consequently, I was confined to an incubator, deprived of my mother's touch, until I could breathe unassisted.

Scientific research emphasizes the importance of immediate post-birth skin-to-skin contact between mother and baby for regulating temperature, breathing, and heart rate. Separated from my mother, I depended on machinery. Beyond these physical benefits, I missed crucial emotional nourishment such as bonding, breastfeeding, and a feeling of security. The absence of immediate care and touch has left a lasting imprint on me, making forming solid interpersonal bonds complex and significantly affecting my emotional development.

My premature birth might have led to cognitive and motor delays, along with predispositions to mental health and neurodevelopmental issues. I was isolated from my mother, surrounded by tubes, and abruptly introduced into a stark, unfamiliar world. Three months after my birth, my mother passed away. Whether it was cancer, heartache, or a blend of both, I'll never know. The inability to hold her child must have been agonizing for her. I often question why it wasn't me. Or why couldn't we have departed together? The love she gave me during gestation has left me wrestling with dependency.

Maternal deprivation refers to the absence or loss of a mother's or primary caregiver's nurturing care during a child's early years. The repercussions of this deprivation have been devastating for me. The void left by my mother's absence has permeated every facet of my life. Growing older and encountering harmful situations and abusive circumstances, both within my family and with those I knew, strangers and predators, the pain of my mother's absence has always left me feeling incomplete.

As a child, I couldn't foresee the magnitude of this tragedy. But now, I understand how maternal deprivation, coupled with my foster family's irresponsibility during my formative years and into adulthood, played a part in my attracting toxic and manipulative individuals into my life. Unbeknownst to me, I harbored survivor's guilt deep within, which was an unconscious desire to die because I felt I didn't deserve to live. I nurtured it with misplaced devotion and loyalty, and my naive worldview only intensified it.

To this day, I wrestle with a profound fear of abandonment. I place unwavering trust in those I form bonds with, giving of myself entirely. Unfortunately, this openness has frequently been taken advantage of. My vulnerability and intense craving for attention, acceptance, and love, no matter how feigned or superficial, mark me as an easy prey.

Growing up in the stark absence of maternal affection, the ensuing wound stubbornly defied the soothing passage of time. My heart longed for a treasure it knew to be irretrievably lost—the comforting touch of a mother's love. The agony of suicidal thoughts and close encounters with death marred my adolescence and early adulthood, leading me to the sterile confines of mental institutions more times than I care to admit. Strangely, I found a semblance of belonging within these cold clinical spaces, even if it was only as a statistical or diagnostic entity.

One might assume that I would have learned to be cautious and to guard my trust, but the opposite was true. My struggle was rooted in my tendency to trust too readily, too deeply. In devaluing myself, I over-looked potential threats—predators ready to exploit my innocence and belief in the goodness of people. Un-knowingly, I made myself a prime target for manipula-tion, and those who claimed to care for my well-being were quick to take advantage.

As I waded through the turbulent waters of ado-lescence, the void left by my mother's absence deep-ened into an unbridgeable chasm. I retreated into a for-tress of solitude, and self-harm became my refuge from a torturous existence. The memory of the first cut re-mains vivid—the pain and the sight of my blood pro-vided a strange, transient relief. This gruesome coping mechanism became my ally against relentless distress. Sometimes, I hoped the blade would transport me to the other side of life, where I imagined my mother wait-ing. It served as a temporary antidote to disappoint-ments and heartbreaks, briefly numbing my emotional pain.

The specter of abandonment and rejection has haunted me constantly, driving me to endure toxic rela-tionships that drained me emotionally and physically. In my pursuit of acceptance, I assumed various roles, of-ten compromising my well-being in the hope of recipro-cated kindness. However, their moral compasses re-peatedly pointed in directions starkly different from mine.

In trying to be all things to all people, I risked my well-being to improve theirs, investing my time, energy, commitment, and trust. I clung to the hope of reciprocation, but these interactions only reaffirmed my deep-seated belief in the unworthiness of love and acceptance. This distorted self-image was a direct result of my mother's absence, leaving an unfillable gap in my life. I sought external validation to fill this void, but it was futile, for only my mother's love could make me feel whole. This led to a destructive and continuous cycle of self-sabotage and self-harm, fueled by survivor's guilt.

The haunting question of why I was allowed to live while my mother wasn't constantly tormented me. I felt like I was living on borrowed time, obliged to embrace life fully in her honor. Yet, despite my best efforts, I was consumed by a sense of inadequacy, failing to meet the expectations I imagined she would have had, not to mention those imposed on me by society. My struggle to honor the life she had sacrificed so much to give me felt futile. My attempts at self-harm and suicide only deepened my sense of guilt and suffering. How could such actions be a fitting tribute to her gift of life? This led to an unending pattern of silent guilt and shame that seemed to intensify with each passing moment.

It wasn't until recent years that I recognized survivor's guilt as the primary catalyst behind my actions and inactions in life. My existence is interwoven from not only my genetic predispositions and neurodiverse traits but also from a complex matrix of external circumstances, influences, environmental factors, and internal battles, all fueled by survivor's guilt. This guilt gave birth to self-hatred and gradually eroded my self-esteem, all set against the backdrop of numerous and ongoing traumas that began in the early hours of an October day nearly half a century ago.

While survivor's guilt doesn't constantly haunt my consciousness, it's a subtle undercurrent, gently influencing my life. When I confront it, I aim to eradicate the toxic threads that would have me believe I was the cause of my mother's untimely death. Sometimes, the strength of rational thought, the clear precision of logic, and a robust and mindful perspective prevail over my emotional wiring, traumatic history, and skewed core beliefs. In my mind's portrait of my mother—crafted from the stories I've heard and the fleeting connections formed during my six months in the womb—I find parallels with Lily Potter, Harry Potter's mother.

In my hopeful moments, when I find myself on the positive swing of life's pendulum, I see similarities between Harry Potter's story and mine. My understanding of Harry's life is mainly superficial, yet I recall being fascinated by the first film in 2001. I sometimes ponder the parallels in our narratives. Our stories are intertwined, each spun from the thread of maternal sacrifice. As fierce as lionesses, our mothers willingly laid down their lives for us. However, the aftermath of these sacrifices resulted in diverging paths.

Harry Potter, indelibly marked by his mother's love, was enveloped in an unseen yet powerful protective shield. Her selfless act resonated within him, a guiding light in the darkest times as if a fragment of her soul lived on in him.

My journey, on the other hand, veered off track. The mark I carry is less a shield and more the damaged remnants of emotional abuse and neglect inflicted by my legal guardian. These scars, perhaps born from resentment of my survival, served as relentless reminders of my turbulent beginnings. It felt as though the ghost of my past was permanently etched within me, casting a long shadow even on the sunniest days.

While Harry found a surrogate family and love with the Weasleys, a beacon of hope in his tumultuous life, I faced fear and abuse from my guardian, a constant whirlwind of dread. The terror instilled in me was akin to the fear that Voldemort spread throughout the wizarding world. However, where Harry faced and overcame his fear, I was left to grapple with mine in isolation.

Despite these challenges, both Harry and I demonstrated remarkable resilience. Harry, with his unwavering courage, confronted his fears directly. Cognitive distortions often obscure my view of this, but despite my trials, I managed to heal many of my old wounds and set out on a new journey under the watchful eye of what seems a celestial guardian.

Intimations of Peril from Being Unheld

Born prematurely into a world of unfulfilled promises
A life begun in the sterile embrace of machines
Deprived of the warmth of a mother's touch
I was left to navigate the labyrinth of existence alone
Haunted by the specter of maternal love, forever out of reach
A phantom limb of the soul, aching in its absence
My heart, a vessel filled with the poison of self-loathing
A bitter draught I drink from daily, a relentless tormentor
The mirror reflects a stranger, a distorted image of self
A puppet dancing on the strings of others' expectations
My life, a stage where I play countless roles
Each one, a mask hiding the raw, unvarnished truth of me
Unsure of the image in the mirror that reflects the face of me
I am a moth drawn to the flame of toxic affection
Burning in the fire of manipulation, yet absurdly yearning for its warmth
The void within me, a chasm carved by the absence of maternal love
A gaping wound, festering with the pus of guilt and regret

I am a survivor, yet I bear the weight of the fallen
A Sisyphus, in an internal inferno, forever pushing the boulder of guilt up the hill of existence
My life, woven threads of despair and hope, filled to the brim with optimistic insistence
A testament to the human spirit's resilience in the face of adversity
Yet, I am a prisoner, shackled by the chains of my past
My hell, a fortress of solitude, built with bricks of self-hatred
I am the architect of my prison, the jailer of my soul
In the silence of my isolation, I hear the reiterations of my lament
Still, I feel in my heart, despite the cavities of despair, a splint of hope
I must believe it's possible to forge a path toward self-acceptance
For I am more than the sum of my past, more than my mistakes and those I've trusted
Strong-willed
Self-determined
Indomitable
Hopeful
Formidable
Hurt, healing, and high-powered
In the end, I realize the key to my freedom lies within me
In the acceptance of my flaws, in the embrace of my pain, bruises, and imperfections,
For it is in the darkness that we find the light

And it is in the breaking of the dawn that the light shines through the ruptures to become whole again

Chapter Two

From the moment my mother succumbed to the cancer that my birth had roused from its dormant state, my closest relative was my maternal grandmother. However, to refer to her as 'grandmother' would undermine the warmth typically associated with the term. In this work, I'll refer to her as my legal guardian or foster mother, both terms technically correct but chosen primarily for their chilly appropriateness. The details of her divorce from my grandfather, a reverend, remain a mystery to me. What I can confirm, however, is that we lived together in a low-income dwelling until I finally fled upon graduating high school at the tender age of seventeen.

Her feelings towards me were as distant as the North Pole is from the South. My great-grandmother whispered stories to me that painted a picture of my guardian as a woman who might have committed murder if she could have evaded both earthly and divine justice. Such allegations might shock those who knew her, but they resonate with my childhood memories. My great-grandmother, Nana, who kept my mother's memory alive with tales, once told me that my guardian had dropped me on my head as an infant. She also recounted an incident when I was left to endure a high fever without medical help.

These stories don't surprise me, considering the neglect I experienced under my guardian's watch. She took me to the doctor only once for mandatory school vaccinations. That was it. There were no dental appointments and no medical care for a painfully limiting and odd-looking defect in both my feet.

Beyond vaccinations, the only medical professional I remember seeing during her care was an optometrist. I believe her motivation for taking me for an eye examination was less about the necessity of glasses and more about finding a means to humiliate me under the pretense of wellness. It's likely this endeavor aimed to have me further stereotyped at school, among the kids in the neighborhood, and at church by getting me a prescription to be a "four eyes."

I was often compared to a popular '90s TV nerd during my pre-teen years. Despite the mockery, I felt a strange kinship with Urkel, who, like me, only wanted to do right by others but was instead ridiculed, misunderstood, and ostracized.

Even now, as an adult, I struggle to prioritize my health. Would you believe that my first visit to a dentist wasn't until I was past twenty-five? Of course, I understand that my health is my responsibility. And although part of the delay was because I didn't have a decent health insurance policy, most of it was because it was tough overcoming the effects of a childhood devoid of health consciousness.

As a child, I couldn't discern whether the stories of neglect were fact or merely fabrications spun by my great-grandmother—a woman who may have harbored resentment for not being granted my custody after my mother's demise. Reflecting on these memories now, bolstered by the wisdom acquired over the years, I can almost certainly confirm the neglectful actions taken against me by my guardian, seemingly because I continued to live while her firstborn daughter did not.

My account is based on my perceptions, and it seems appropriate to begin with her values. A devout churchgoer, she served as a deaconess. Her reputation and appearance held great significance to her. Caring for me, her orphaned grandchild, was a badge of honor that elevated her status in others' eyes. Yet, from where I stood, she was no different from any other indifferent foster mother reaping financial rewards. It appeared beyond her ability, even as a God-fearing church official, to show unconditional love toward the one she regarded as her beloved's killer.

She had a penchant for the Lincoln Town Car and the status it bestowed upon her. This, coupled with her addiction to Pepsi, shaped how she cared for me. I remember her denying me access to driver's education in high school, fearing a rise in insurance premiums. This choice, frustrating but seemingly trivial at the time, proved to have enduring implications for my life and contributed to why, even after finally getting my driver's license after turning 18, I plan to never sit behind the wheel of a car again. By my teenage years, another incident involving the car occurred, but I was mainly fending for myself since the car payments and her addiction owned her exclusively.

Unaware of premiums or financing, I grew to become aware that she earned an income working as a transporter at a hospital and received a state stipend for my relative foster care. Despite this, we lived in near poverty, our lives dictated by her car and Pepsi addiction. The fridge was often empty, save for a 2-liter bottle of soda, prioritized over food. At that time, I was unaware of how addictions can cloud a person's sense of responsibility and diminish their self-control, as I understand now. As a child, I perceived these actions as deliberate displays of selfishness and cruelty.

From an outsider's perspective, our struggles might have seemed primarily rooted in financial hardship rather than malicious intent or hatred. And perhaps there's some validity to that notion. As most of us carry some cognitive biases, it might be challenging to accept that a grandmother, a respected church official, could harbor such darkness. However, my nearly half-century of memories and experiences narrate a different tale. I'm here to share the truth as I lived it, perceived it, and understood it. Naturally, I cannot claim to know with absolute certainty the true intentions or motives behind my foster mother's actions during our shared existence in that two-bedroom, second-floor tenement. Therefore, I would not stake my existence on the complete accuracy of my assertions and assumptions about this woman.

But taking into account secondhand tales, the memory of the continuous trauma still embedded in my physiology, and my current cognitive ability, I can surmise that my legal guardian did everything in her power to break me from the moment she was granted custodian of my welfare until I escaped at seventeen. I was an unwanted orphan, used as a pawn to maintain her socioeconomic status, nurture her vanity, uphold her religious facade, secure peer support, and exact cruel revenge.

Shards of a Shattered Innocence

In the cradle of youth, where love should have bloomed
A garden, wilted, under a heartlessly imposed desire
A child's laughter, silenced too soon

Echoes in the gloomy rooms filled with vindictive intent
Touched cold as winter
Fed a bitter nectar of accusatory resent
A fever's rage, no healing loom
In the shadow of neglect, innocence is consumed,
Debris of caregiving mistakes and misgivings fell, swept
up with a psychotropic broom
In the church's glow veiled with hypocrisy
A guardian's love, a deceptive perfume
Draws in attention and disturbs responsibilities
Lulling into deceptive acceptance and helpless submis-
sion
Masking the pain, a childhood's wounds swell invisibly
Like a silent prayer into the nocturnal reigns of the day
A mother's sacrifice, an ethereal safeguard
Impress on the soul, a hope in the fabric of a survivor's
gloom
A pawn in the game of a guardian's ruse
A facade of faith in the shards of a shattered innocence
When will the phoenix rise in immense suppleness?
Centuries of hurt, in God's name
Still echoing in philharmonic halls with a poignant re-
frain
As the heart's orchestra plays a solemn song
There was a way out, but no way to know, being so un-
derdeveloped
Love didn't know his name
Time was making its acquaintance progressively
Strength was unmistakable
Whether he knew it or not, his resilience was inherent
and emerging inadvertently

Chapter Three

My great-grandmother was a radiant chapter in the complex narrative of my life. She embedded in me a profound understanding of the mind's immense power, almost as if it were a prophetic prelude to my future embrace of the hermetic philosophy that proclaims, "All is mind." Like gentle whispers in the wind, her stories echoed my mother's spirit, keeping her essence alive within me. Each narrative reverberated with her regret for not being granted my guardianship.

Her confession was profoundly moving, revealing that my mother's dying wish had been for her to become my guardian. But it wasn't only her poignant memories that fortified my understanding of the mind's profound influence on one's life.

She resided alone in a three-bedroom, two-story house on the city's northern side for as long as I can remember. Almost every Christmas, she gifted me basics like underwear or socks from Hanes or Fruit of the Loom or some sweater. She baked the most divine lemon meringue pies I've ever savored.

There's a humorous encounter with my Nana that remains etched in my memory, even as many other cherished moments have slipped away due to accidental head injuries. My grasp of the concept of oral fixation has always been minimal, and as a child, I was certainly unfamiliar with its clinical terminology. Yet, an oral fixation has had a firm hold on me, unconstrained by age or time. I found myself sucking my thumb well past the age deemed typical for children.

I recall her issuing a threat, suggesting she would smear her dog's waste on my thumb to put an end to my incessant habit. I cannot definitively say whether she would have followed through with this unpalatable act. Although I was old enough to have outgrown thumb-sucking, I was too naive to understand the art of bluffing.

Her words, possibly empty, were potent enough to curb my habit, albeit temporarily. Because I reverted to this familiar comfort intermittently during my teenage years and even adulthood. These were brief episodes, fleeting moments to satisfy an oral fixation that has stubbornly persisted.

I distinctly remember a photograph of my great-grandmother and me when I was just a toddler, her figure stooped over me, her face hidden behind tinted glasses, a smile that seemed to announce, "Cheese! Look at us. We're simply perfect together!" Time, however, is relentless. As the years passed, her body could no longer stoop that low.

By the time my 20s were blossoming, osteoporosis had taken hold of her body, forcing her to move from her primary upstairs bedroom to the solitude of the first floor in the dining room. Throughout my youth, her movements transitioned from being assisted by a cane to eventually using a wheelchair. Her arthritis made lemon pie-making a struggle, but the strength of her cognitive function allowed her to channel the spirit of Thomas Edison. She fashioned a variety of makeshift gadgets to perform tasks her body could no longer execute with ease.

Another memorable moment, rich with humor, was when she confessed her admiration for Jay-Z. An interview she watched on her console television, housed in an elegant wooden cabinet, ignited her appreciation not for the musician but for the businessman and self-made man. This sentiment inspired a new-found respect within me for the hip-hop star.

Living in her home after my high school graduation, we experienced many beautiful moments. I hadn't yet reached 18, making the temporary living arrangements outside the confines of the law, given that my foster mother still held legal guardianship over me. Nonetheless, my Nana's home served as more than just a shelter; it became a sanctuary during the few months I resided there.

Our cohabitation wasn't always harmonious, but the intermittent discord only added depth to the symphony of our shared life. It was a welcome contrast to the grim environment I was a refugee from.

The most impactful intersection of our lives was her proclamation that the one possession no one could ever take from her was her mind. Amidst family upheavals and the relentless decline of her body over time, she remained steadfast. She insisted that even if nature claimed her health or her family disputed her estate, no force could strip her of her mental strength or competence. To me, this stood as her enduring legacy.

If a man's mind can be likened to a womb—nurturing any seeds planted within—then my guardian's neglectful and abusive words and actions were akin to invasive intrusions into my psyche. Their effects bore within me offspring of emotional deformity, born from an affair that could be analogously described as 'incestuous.' This term is not used to denote the biological implications of close kinship but rather to emphasize the violation of my mental sanctity. The criminality of the act lies not in the relational closeness but in the non-consensual invasion of my 'private part'—my mind.

My great-grandmother, despite her advanced years, could provide me little sanctuary from the torment of my toxic relationship with my guardian. Indeed, by the time I summoned the courage to reveal the depth of my distress, the influence of my guardian had already established deep roots in my life. I could see the stir of frustration in my Nana's eyes, a silent admission of her limitations as the recipient of my woeful tale. It lingered in the air, a palpable sadness, a quiet indictment of the helpless situation we found ourselves in, a sorrowful reflection of her own granddaughter's fate.

Had my mother been aware of the trials I was fated to endure, might she have reconsidered her loving sacrifice? Like a raven perched ominously on the periphery of my consciousness, this rhetorical question has whispered a haunting, echoing lament for most of my life.

Whispers of Nana from Time's Tapestry

She was so sweet
Physically limited
Mentally agile
Home kept neat

She was a storyteller
Kept my mother alive
Smile so warm
Geriatrics, an impetuous dweller

A baker of pastries
Lover of reminiscences
Demonstrative of mind over matter
Whispers of whimsical anecdotal tapestries

A prisoner to her ailments
Gifting under garments wrapped in festive paper
Sugar-coated memories
Treasurer of our shared time spent

A legacy left behind
Holding on despite all and the one
Triggers pulled, ricochet
Impenetrable power of the mind

Chapter Four

Worldwide, dogs and cats—beings that unashamedly urinate in public and openly groom themselves—often receive more affection than I have in around 39% of my life. This is a result of enduring years of incessant, insidious neglect and emotional torment as a motherless child, left to the mercy of my legal guardian. You might wonder how such abuse could continue undetected.

I've previously touched on her precarious care during my infancy, the glaring lack of medical attention, her addiction and the subsequent effects on my well-being, and the impact of her vanity and narcissism, particularly concerning her automobile. To fully understand the numerous ways she emotionally and psychologically violated me, we must revisit her faith. Each person's relationship with their God is deeply personal, an intimacy that cannot be stolen. However, it was her faith that she brandished as a weapon of fear and a tool for planting seeds of destruction.

I was unaware at the time of the damage being inflicted. Only in recent years have I begun piecing together the fragments of my past. Around the age of 10 or 11, I was molested by a babysitter during a summer visit with my father. I understand I should not blame myself, but when faced with the unfortunate or adversity, my initial reaction is to examine my culpability. Being raised in an environment where I was persistently accused and blamed for my mother's death, it's not surprising that I developed a pattern of default self-blame, even in the face of traumatic events.

While the exact causes of many mental health conditions are still uncertain, common risk factors have been identified, including genetic predisposition, environmental influences, and abnormalities in brain chemistry. I believe my premature birth predisposed me to my mental health and neurodevelopmental disorders. However, the sexual assault I experienced, a violation of my trust, might have also played a role. However, due to my psychosocial malnourishment at the time— craving attention from the one person I wanted it from the most—I sometimes feels as though I might have invited the babysitter's actions in some way.

That same year, at a time I can't recall, I woke up abruptly in the quiet of the night. I sat up straight, my gaze drawn to the foot of my bed. In the dim light, two nebulous figures floated, their shapes resembling phallic symbols, one as dark as obsidian, the other as pale as moonlight. A scream struggled to escape my throat, but all that filled the silence was the sound of my feet hitting the cold floor as I ran from the spectral figures.

I sought help from my guardian but heard her rhythmic snoring and didn't try to wake her. Glancing back into my room from the threshold, the ghostly figures were still there. Could their presence have been a manifestation of my subconscious fears or suppressed shame from the babysitter's actions?

Driven by curiosity as inexplicable as it was intense, I watched the apparitions drift towards me, mirroring the tide of fear surging through my veins. I withdrew to the living room, my heart pounding against my ribcage. A woman's voice called my name, a phantom whisper in the silence, but my guardian's snores still filled the air. I knew it wasn't her speaking.

The terror was palpable, yet it held a sense of wonder, a fascination with the unknown. I found myself curled up on the sofa, my body instinctively assuming a fetal position as if to protect me from the night's horrors. The fear saturated my bones, causing me to tremble until sleep eventually took hold.

After a few hours, morning light finally seeped through the opaque curtains of the living room window, bathing my surroundings in a warm glow. As I awoke, the night's events felt like fragments of a dream. The night's occurrences still unsettled me, but I questioned, "Was it all a dream?"

The phallic apparitions, the woman's voice—were these all symbols of a psychological amalgamation of traumatized thoughts and disarray? Could they have been a reflection of my inner chaos, an embodiment of my struggle to come to terms with the sexual assault? The answers remained elusive, concealed within the maze of my subconscious, waiting to be deciphered through the interpretation of my dream.

However, it couldn't have been a dream, for how else would I have ended up in the living room? Based on my knowledge of sleepwalking, one remains unaware of one's actions during such states. Therefore, I couldn't have been asleep. In my bewilderment, I sought comfort and clarification from my guardian. My mind was fertile soil, and she grasped the chance to retaliate for the perceived "murder" of her daughter. She told me the experience I had was divine retribution. I was a sinner, a monstrosity in need of repentance. I was a heathen, and that was the justification.

Maybe my admission of auditory and visual hallucinations didn't surprise her. Perhaps she was familiar with such phenomena. Or, there was the possibility that these were genuine spirits, demons, ghosts, or other entities from the supernatural or paranormal realm. Could the woman's voice have been my mother reaching out from beyond? These were the ideas I considered as I attempted to understand the experience. My guardian was the only person I could turn to, the only one who could help me comprehend the terror that had seized me so profoundly. Reflecting on it now, it could have been the onset of psychosis and the emergence of the mental disorders that would later take hold in my life.

Yet, none of these fears compared to the fear of God that now pulsed through me. I was a transgressor for causing my mother's death and a sinner for the sexual assault. From that moment, a quiet self-loathing began to take root.

The determination of this woman made her actions insidious. Regardless of what she did or said that made me feel insignificant and non-existent, I believed I deserved it. My life post-departure from her home would be filled with the same feelings of unworthiness of love. Moreover, even after my death, I presumed Satan would claim my soul for torment. I felt damned for merely being born, with no hope of redemption for my sins, unless I surrendered to a God I believed concurred with His earthly representative and also viewed me as an abomination. I didn't feel worthy of Christ's sacrifice on the cross.

The Veiled Dance with Phantoms

It's always my fault
I'm the one to blame
I'm the reason for my failure
I've attracted all the misfortune into my life
All the toxic relationships
Each economic fluctuation
Every event that has precipitated on my terrestrial life
Have they been from currents of thoughts I've un-
leashed into the wind?
The gravitational pull of misery that holds me confined
to the earth
A natural law, immutable
Yet my ability
My emotional agility
That's within my capacity and power to change
Yet I have the audacity to hope for something for which
I'm unworthy
Mercy
Compassion
Care
Love
My heart spent years in the aftermath, still searching
In my tweens, in my twenties, in my thirties
Those men took something from me that had yet to be
solidified
She injected in me a poison that corrupted my core be-
lief system
A dogma built on love was presented as confirmation
that I'm forever the blame

My guardian's grief and irreplaceable loss
The dark side of the universe basking in the delight of
my self-directed disdain and dilapidation
For years, I wanted my life to end
I didn't deserve it
Everything is my fault
I'm the one to blame
Even through the egoism and erroneous nature of my
justification for the trajectory of my life
All I could see was the ownership of my fate
God the infallible had made a mistake
To make things right, He was bestowing upon me a life
no person would want to live
But I know different intellectually
But I'm still trying to uproot the malignant growths spir-
itually of the truth
The phantoms hover still at the foot of my bed
I still hear the woman's voice calling to me
But the fear won't penetrate my heart
I'm welcoming only thoughts of liberation, acceptance,
and love in my head

Chapter Five

If the individual whose care for me was financed by the state held no affection for me, how could I justify loving myself? When I approached her with the account of my terrifying night, shivering under the potential yet undiagnosed onset of mental illness, she could not summon even a fragment of empathy or a compassionate question about my welfare from her narcissistic and vindictive heart. Yet, she found the capacity to label me a devilish monstrosity, asserting I merited my predicament. I had not, at that time, distanced myself from the anthropomorphic image of God, which I have since done, and I couldn't dismiss the feeling that even the creator of the boundless universe had abandoned me despite His supposed unconditional love for all.

As I've grown older and evolved spiritually, I've learned to appreciate the beauty in my mother's sacrifice. However, for the longest time, I nurtured the mistaken belief that my mother wished to leave me. This belief originated from the initial weeks of birth when I lay connected to tubes in an incubator, deprived of her touch and the reassuring rhythm of her heartbeat. I was left to battle for my survival rather than being nestled in her arms. I used to presume she foresaw my future disappointments and that her retreat into oblivion was a form of avoidance.

My father was an inconsistent figure in my life, leaving me feeling abandoned. To this day, relationships with men, whether they be familial, fraternal, or professional, frighten me due to the multiple sexual assaults I've endured over the years. Yet, paradoxically, I find myself craving male companionship in the forms of father figures, close friendships, and role models.

There came a day when I was a young boy, a day of such profound yearning for my father, that I found myself sneaking to the kitchen while my guardian slept to dial 911. My voice shook as I asked them to bring my father to me, hoping to bridge the gaping disconnect between us. Tears streamed down my face as I pleaded into the phone, my voice echoing in the silent night.

Suddenly, the familiar creak of my foster mother's bedroom door pierced the quiet. I hurriedly hung up the phone, my heart racing. My act, innocent and desperate, was a plea for the sporadic masculine and paternal energy that was glaringly missing from my life. It ignited a fury in my guardian, who now had to deal with the embarrassing task of explaining to the officer that there was no emergency.

In my youthful innocence, I hadn't realized that abruptly ending a call from a distraught eight-year-old boy pleading for his father would prompt a call back from the authorities. She punished me until I was a sobbing, quivering child for daring to reach out. As I lay alone in my room, the welts on my young body throbbing in rhythm with my heartbeat, my ears still ringing with her harsh reproof, a pattern was ingrained into my psyche: men, whether directly like the babysitter or indirectly through the punishment for my attempt to contact my father, were bringers of pain and suffering.

Much like a meticulous gardener, my guardian nurtured her seedlings with the searing rays of her glaring disdain, saturating them in a downpour of demoralizing words and feeding them with the decay of validation and support. She would whisper in my ear, a cold wind, that love would always be out of my reach, that friendship was a luxury I couldn't afford, especially after the neighborhood bullies had their way with me.

I've spun through life, a paradox in motion. For many years, I've labeled myself an "intelligent idiot." Partly jesting when I would utter the phrase in casual conversations to incite a laugh, I reveled in the illusion that the alliteration was a unique badge of self-deprecation I bestowed upon myself. Yet, recently, I've realized that this title was an involuntary echo of my guardian's craftily woven insinuations that I possessed "book sense but not common sense."

This seed flourished under her guardianship, soaking in the sunlight of her scorn and drawing deeply from her well of contempt. I am beginning to uncover the truth that many of the core beliefs I've held onto are not genuinely mine. Each dismissal of my emotions, each persistent denial of validation, each withholding of affection, was a stab to my heart. I was constantly reminded of my inadequacy, lack of intellect, and unlovability.

These words, these actions, they fed my survivor's guilt, eating at me from within, a silent predator. I was convinced that I was the personification of the vile words my guardian spouted, for why else would someone who was meant to love me hurt me so deeply? Although I'm bringing awareness to these faulty thought patterns, I'm still trapped daily in a cycle of subconscious self-blame and self-loathing, a process that has stuck to me, a persistent shadow, even decades after escaping her care.

Now, as an adult, I find myself echoing her treatment of me, sometimes with even greater severity. I have internalized my guardian's poisonous messages and continue to carry these harmful beliefs about myself. The external source of torment may have disappeared, but the internal scars remain. Her voice has transformed into my own—resounding, "I'm worthless.

I'm a nobody. No one could ever like me. People will always use me. I'm pathetic. I'm a burden. I'm nothing special."

Unearthing Love

Where is the love?
Why must my heart break in the silence of the night?
Why do I still feel like that little boy?
I only wanted her love
I only wanted to be wanted
I only wanted to be appreciated
Now, tossed about with the flimsiest of foundations
I try to reprogram the defective algorithms that have biologically and circumstantially been put into operation
I'm digging deep
Traversing the vast terrain of my psyche and soul to unearth what will lead to self-love
What right do I have to want happiness?
That's what I used to think
As I sank in deluded thoughts that pushed me to the brink of my sanity
Now I'm in recovery
Trying to unearth love
Pushing egoism aside, I see I'm no one special
There may have been special conditions and circumstances
But at some point, we have to say, 'Enough is enough'
I don't want to cry

I don't want to hurt anymore
Just as the sun rises and stars are suspended above
It's time to put in the work
Accept me as I am
Accept the truth and unearth love

Chapter Six

I yearned to resent my guardian for her mistreatment, but how could I condemn someone for inflicting upon me what, at that time, I believed I deserved? Society ingrains the concept of punitive consequences for wrongdoings. Being a living being, the sole victor in a race of 525 billion sperm, I took on the blame for my foster mother's severity, viewing it as my due. How could I express my complaints to God when He seemed to side with her? At least, so I believed. I thought I deserved the theft of my innocence, the isolation, the bullying. Yet, paradoxically, I didn't feel deserving of the praise bestowed upon me for being a "special" child, an intellectual prodigy. The honor roll, the awards, the lead roles in plays, the solos in choral concerts, and the admiration from my teachers should have acted as positive reinforcement, as a beacon highlighting the falsehoods in my perceptions and beliefs. Yet, they only served to deepen my confusion.

These teachers, who spent mere hours with me each day, seemed to care for me more than the woman I believed should have cherished me the most. The support from these strangers, unfamiliar yet caring, was exhilarating. The validation I received was a salve to my wounded spirit. Knowing I was special motivated me to strive even harder for their commendation. The pendulum swing from an environment of stark indifference to one of compassion was emotionally taxing. I longed for my guardian's interest in my accomplishments and yearned for her admiration, similar to the respect I received from my teachers. Eventually, after numerous futile attempts to win her affection, I accepted the harsh truth: her love was an elusive dream, and no amount of approval from teachers or my peers' parents could replace it.

I remember a day when I was 13. I had to stay after school, and she didn't come to pick me up. One of my teachers drove me home, bending the rules to do so. Perhaps she saw the desolation in my eyes and felt the chaos within me. As I was about to leave her car, she handed me a cassette tape featuring Mariah Carey's "Hero." I will forever be indebted to that middle school teacher for her intervention. As I listened to that uplifting song on loop, I grew a lasting fondness for Mariah and a perpetual love for the melody.

However, when the final note ceased, the depressive bouts would return, dragging me back into a world laden with reminders and triggers. My guardian's hostility originated from her viewing me as a reminder—of her daughter, her illness, her death, and the immense void left in her existence. "Hurt people hurt people," I've been told, and she was a prisoner to her bitterness and fury. I have forgiven her. Yet, I wish she could have absolved me, despite my unintended role in my mother's death. My birth might have precipitated her end, but my mother's decision was not my fault. My mother chose to risk her life to give me mine, to leave a part of her in the world. Surely, my guardian, a follower of Christ, could comprehend such selfless love. However, it was unfair to make me feel as though I was the one "child of God" unworthy of salvation through the sacrificial blood of the Son of God.

Every element of my life, directly or indirectly, is marked by the indelible stamp of survivor's guilt. This unshakeable phantom has insidiously woven itself into the vital intricacies of my existence, coursing through the veins of my life with the inexorability of a lifetime's blood flow. It gnaws at the pillars of my mental well-being and infiltrates my vital organs—subtly slicing, relentlessly shredding, and insidiously dicing from within. This pervasive siege permeates my entire being, imperceptibly yet profoundly, echoing the hermetic axiom from the Kybalion, 'As above, so below.' It's as if she had nurtured me for an entire year on baby formula laced with shards of finely ground glass, each innocent sip inflicting silent devastation.

What has made things so rough in my life are reminders and triggers of trauma. Every misfortune, every
setback, every toxic relationship, every failure, every re-
fill of psychiatric medication, every depressive episode,
every anxious thought, every night alone, every substance misused, every day without a call or text, every
vulnerable moment, every rejection are triggers and reminders.

From the moment of my conception, I've been
fighting for survival. I survived premature birth. I survived emotional abuse and neglect. I survived bullying. I
survived heartbreak. I survived multiple sexual assaults.
I survived physical assaults. I survived immense loss. I
survived scandal. I survived homelessness. I survived
unemployment. I survived betrayal. I survived multiple
acts of self-harm. I survived drug misuse. I survived numerous suicide attempts. I survived abandonment. I
survived manipulation. I survived exploitation. I survived multiple car accidents. I survived illness. I survived
failure. I survived disappointment. I survived lonesome-
ness. I survived being held psychologically hostage. I
survived conspiracy and so much more!

I'm on a continual and upward spiritual path.
Yet, no matter how much I've grown, I've yet to survive
survivor's guilt, and it is a nuanced, surreptitious invasion into each fundamental area of my life, in blatant
and subtle ways. But as my great-grandmother showed,
I know that with the power of my mind to correct each
faulty algorithm, the day will eventually come when I

can say I survived this, too, because I've finally caught a glimpse of the truth. A hero lies within me.

Melodies in the Echo Chamber

do-re-me-fa-so-la-ti-do
Doleful memories all within my physiology
Remnants of a mother's love that I thought I didn't de-
serve
do-re-me-fa-so-la-ti-do
Memorizing subconsciously the lies that I would bring to
light
Far away it was taken, kept hidden and forsaken, but
now my mind has awakened to the truth
do-re-me-fa-so-la-ie-do
Sowing seeds of love, hope, peace, and prosperity to ob-
scure growths from seeds of destruction
Languishing no more because there is a divine light
within that is my essence
do-re-me-fa-so-la-ti-do
Temporal passions and fixated notions all seek to put
me to sleep and darken my shine
But, does not the lotus sprout up from the muck?
do-re-me-fa-so-la-ti-do

R. Antonio Matta

Author ▫ Poet ▫ Artist

Check out my books, audiobooks, and digital stories!

www.rantoniomatta.com

Other works:
- *Your Genesis*
- *Destiny's Stereo*
- *Love Is in the Eye of the Beholder*
- *7 Key Ways to Unlock the Infinite Potential of Your Therapy Practice with Digital Content*